Galilee Fishermen

alilee
ILEE

th

ffa

Nomad Shepherds

TEN TOWN COUNTRY

Jericho

Jordan River

Caravan from the East

PERAEA

ALT SEA

Philadelphia

special introduction and summary
by Chris Spencer

© 1980 David C. Cook Publishing Co.
850 N. Grove Ave.
Elgin, IL 60120
All rights reserved
ISBN: 0-89191-285-1

Published 1980 by World Distributors (Manchester) Limited
A Member of The Pentos Group
PO Box 111, 12 Lever Street, Manchester M60 1TS
Designed and produced for World Distributors (Manchester) Limited by
Asset Publishing Limited
Copyright © 1980 Asset Publishing Limited
Printed in Italy

The Stories Jesus Told
The Prodigal Son

written by Heather Dyer
illustrated by Bernard Brett

Jesus was a wonderful storyteller, as you will see if you read through the Gospels — the first four books of the New Testament. But his stories, which are called parables, were not told just for people to listen to and enjoy. There were deeper meanings to them, and lessons to be learned from each one. Through his parables — and through his whole teaching — Jesus was showing us what God is like and how important it is for us to trust God and to follow the example Jesus was setting for us.

In his parables Jesus always talked about things that anyone could understand—the things everyone would find around them. He spoke of sheep, farms, fish, seeds, bread, fruit, money, to mention but a few. And when he told his parables everyone listened, for he spoke in a else. You can read about how he did this in some of the parables in this series.

THE YOUNG MAN walked down the dusty road. He was on his way to the big city many miles away. He was very excited for he was setting out on an adventure, his pockets bulging with money. He was rich, he was free, and he was going to enjoy himself. If he had thought to look back, he would have seen his father standing by the doorway of his house, two big tears trickling down his face as he watched the son who seemed to have forgotten him already.

The father turned sadly back into the house where life was going on as usual. The servants were busy about their jobs, sweeping the floors, fetching water from the well, and minding the animals on the farm. His

elder son seemed happy as he worked in the fields, which one day would now all belong to him. If only his younger son had been happy and content to live and work on the farm, too. Once again the father thought of the talk they had had some weeks before.

"Father, when you die, will you divide all the things you own between my brother and me?"

"Yes," his father had replied. "You shall have your share."

"Well then," his younger son had said, "do you mind if I have my share now? If I wait until you die, I may be quite an old man myself. I should like my part now while I am young and can enjoy it."

His father had felt very sad when he heard that. But because he was a kind father and wanted his son to be happy, he had divided his property and given his young son the part that would be his.

The elder brother was angry. He thought his brother was stupid and greedy, and he was cross with him for making their father so sad. But the younger son was selfish and thought only of himself. Before many days were up, he had sold the fields and animals that now belonged to him, put a few clothes in a bag, the money in his pocket, and set out on the road to adventure.

He whistled as he walked along the road. He was thinking of the things he was going to buy and the exciting things he was going to do.

When he reached the city at last, he was more excited than ever. He bought himself some fine new clothes and went to the most expensive places to eat.

When the other young men and women he met saw how much money he had to spend, they soon made friends with him. They helped him spend his money in very foolish ways and in doing all sorts of things that were wrong. His money was disappearing very quickly. One morning he suddenly found it had all gone.

He went to his newfound friends to see if they would lend him some money while he went to look for a job. But when they found he had no money left, they were not friendly anymore. He was all alone in the big city.

Just to make things worse, a great famine came to the land, and there was little to eat. What food there was cost a lot of money so there was none for a young man who could not afford to pay for it. So he went into the country where a farmer took pity on him and said he would pay him a little if he looked after his pigs.

The young man was so hungry he would have done anything to earn some money to buy food. In fact he even thought of taking the bean pods he could see the pigs eating in the dusty farmyard.

As he sat among the fields he thought for the first time of his father's farm.

How stupid I am, he thought. *Here I am starving when my father's servants have all they want to eat and more besides. I will go back to my father and say, 'Father, I have done wrong to God and to you. Even though you may not wish to think of me as your son anymore, please let me come home to work as a servant.'*

So that same day the young man got up and started on the long journey home.

At home the old father had never forgotten his son. Every day he climbed the steps to the flat roof of the house to see if he could see his son coming home. Each day he came down again looking a little sadder and a little older.

But one day when he looked out he saw someone far away in the distance coming toward the house. The old man squinted his eyes against the sun and looked hard at the man. Then his heart began to beat more quickly, and his hands began to tremble with excitement.

"It is my son!" he said, and he ran as quickly as he could out of the house and down the road to meet him.

The young son was limping along the stony road in his bare feet. His shoes had worn out long ago, and his clothes were all tattered. He felt so ashamed when he saw his father welcoming him with open arms.

"Father," he said, "I'm sorry. I have done wrong in

God's sight and in yours. . . ." But his father did not let him finish. He flung his arms around him and led him into the house.

"Bring the best clothes you can find." he called to the servants, "and put them on my son. Put a ring on his finger and find him some shoes. Then go and prepare a splendid meal for we must have a welcome home party."

So the servants went and did as they were told. Soon
the whole house was full of excitement. Everyone began
to sing and dance, and then they all sat down to enjoy the
fine meal that had been prepared.

The elder son was still working in the fields. When he heard the sound of music and merrymaking, he wondered what all the noise was about.

"Your brother has returned!" one of the servants called out. When he heard this, the elder brother was very angry and came running toward the house. But he would not go in and join the fun. His father went out to speak to him.

"Why all the fuss?" the elder son asked. "You haven't given a party for me, and I've stayed with you all my life."

"Please come and join us," his father replied. "Don't be cross. You know that everything here belongs to you now. Of course I am happy to have you always with me. But surely you must know how happy I am to have the son I had lost and thought might even be dead, back home again."

He put an arm around each of the sons he loved so dearly, and they went into the house together.

In this parable Jesus was teaching that God cares very much for those who are in need of help. This is shown by the fact that even though the prodigal (or wasteful) son thinks only of himself, his father never stops loving him and receives him home with great joy. The father even runs to greet his son. This is a picture of how eager God is to welcome all who turn to him for forgiveness and help.

The elder son in the parable is a picture of the proud church leaders, who were disgusted that Jesus should mix with people who had fallen into all sorts of bad ways. Through this parable Jesus was teaching that God will welcome anyone who comes to him.

Where Jesus Told His Stories

Acr

N

Carmel M

Caesarea

SAMARIA

Joppa

The Good Sama

THE GREAT SEA

Gaza

Christ Preaching

Jerusalem

St. John
Preaching

Bethlehem
Masada